Object Lessons
for
Children's Worship

Mary Foxwell Loeks

BAKER BOOK HOUSE
Grand Rapids, Michigan

The following publishers have given permission to quote Scripture references from their copyrighted material:

Berk.   — The Modern Language Bible, The Berkeley Version © 1959, 1969 by Zondervan Publishing House, Grand Rapids, Michigan.
RSV   — The Revised Standard Version, © 1946, 1952, 1971, 1973 by the Division of Christian Education of the National Council of the Churches of Christ in the United States of America.
NEB   — The New English Bible, © 1961, 1970 by The Delegates of the Oxford University Press and The Syndics of the Cambridge University Press.
NIV   — The New International Version, © 1978 New York International Bible Society, by the Zondervan Corporation, Grand Rapids, Michigan.
LB   — The Living Bible, © 1971 by Tyndale House Publishers, Wheaton, Illinois.

Verses marked KJV are taken from the King James Version.

ISBN: 0-8010-5584-9

Twelfth printing, September 1995

Printed in the United States of America

To the boys and girls
of Christ Church, Grand Rapids, Michigan;
from whom I have learned so very much

Preface

My father, Philip Foxwell, is a master in the use of the object lesson, so as a young child I came to see its value for communicating biblical principles. Of course, many object lessons and analogies break down if forced too far, for there are no perfect parallels to spiritual truth. Nevertheless, an object lesson is an attempt—if a fallible one—to turn an otherwise abstract concept into something vivid, something that the listener can touch, taste, or smell.

Over the years, I have been exposed to many fine teachers and other highly creative individuals. I have gleaned from them all, and I suspect that I have very few totally original thoughts! The object lessons presented in this book have been culled from my experience and my memory. Where I have been able, I have credited those people whose ideas I have used. (I trust, however, that each of these lessons has its own flavor.)

The object lessons may be used alone, perhaps as a children's sermon. Or, the entire lesson, complete with songs, Bible verse, Bible story, and activity, may be used for children's church or Sunday school. In many cases, the object lesson would also work well with Scripture passages other than the one suggested.

I recommend typing each Bible verse on 3 × 5 cards to distribute to the children, so they can work on it at home. I also advise some sort of follow-up, to see if the children are memorizing the verse and understanding its implications for their lives.

For your convenience, the lessons have been placed under the following headings: God's World; God's Word; God Deals With Sin; Jesus, God's Son; God and His People; The Holy Spirit; The Church and Missions. May you find joy in helping the children around you learn to love and worship our great, triune God!

Mary Foxwell Loeks

Contents

God and His People

The Holy Spirit

The Church and Missions

God's World

1

An Expression of Praise to God

Suggested Songs:

"This Is My Father's World"; "O Who Can Make a Flower?"; The Doxology; "Fairest Lord Jesus"; "All Things Bright and Beautiful"

Bible Verse:

"Let everything he has made give praise to him" Ps. 148:5a, LB.

Objects:

Wild flowers, or some appropriate natural objects. (It would be ideal if you could pick, or find enough, for each child to take one home.)

I was walking through a field near my house yesterday. Way out in the middle of the field I found these wild flowers. Aren't they pretty? Do you know, the tall grass was growing up around the flowers so I could hardly see them until I was almost on top of them. When people plant flowers in their yards or gardens, they water them and take care of them. But I don't think anyone even knew these flowers were there until I found them. Anyone except God, that is! Who made these flowers, Joanie? That's right; God did. And who took care of them, and gave them rainwater and sunshine? God did.
Let me ask you the question that came to my mind when I found these beautiful wild flowers yesterday. Why do you suppose God put them in

the middle of a field, surrounded by tall grass, where people aren't likely to find them? (See if children have any ideas.) God knew these flowers were there, didn't He? The idea that came to me was that God must have put these flowers there to praise Him, and to bring glory and pleasure to Himself. Oh, I know flowers can't praise God in the same way people can, but the psalm from which today's Bible verse comes says that everything God has made can give praise to Him. Let me read it to you now. If you have your Bibles, you can turn to Psalm 148. (Read Ps. 148, I suggest from the Living Bible.) "Let everything he has made give praise to Him!" These flowers helped *me* praise God, because they reminded me of the One who made them! You may each take one of the flowers home with you when you leave today, to help you praise God.

Related Bible Story:

Genesis 1; Psalm 148. The creation of the universe. God made everything in order to bring glory to Himself. Only people were made able to *choose* whether or not they will praise God, and bring glory to Him. What do you choose? (A flannelgraph would be a big help in telling this story. If you do not have access to one, cut pictures from magazines—or draw some—and paste them on six sheets of construction paper, so you have an illustration of the things created on each of the six days.)

Activity: Take a walk.

See how many things you can find that God made. Each child should, if possible, bring one of the items back with him. Otherwise he should be prepared to tell the group one thing he saw. When you come back inside, have each child share the thing he found. Praise God together for all the beautiful, wonderful things He has made.

God's Word

2

A Mirror

Suggested Songs:

"Holy Bible, Book Divine"; "Jesus Loves Even Me"

Bible Verse:

"How can a young man stay pure? By reading your Word and following its rules" Ps. 119:9, LB.

Objects:

A bright colored jam or jelly, smeared on the face of the teacher or leader; a mirror; a wet washcloth.

(As soon as the teacher or leader appears with the jelly on his or her face, there will undoubtedly be comments by the children. He or she can respond with statements such as, "You must be mistaken—there couldn't be jelly on *my* face"; or, "Adults don't go around with jelly on their faces!")
We are going to use some mirrors today. (Display mirror, but make a special point not to look into it.) Can anyone tell me what a mirror is used for? What kind of a job does a mirror do? That's right, Michelle, a mirror shows a person what he looks like. What's that, Sam? You think *I* should look in the mirror? (Look in mirror) Sam, you were right about

my needing to look in the mirror. I seem to have jelly all over my face! I think it would be a good idea if I washed it off! (Do so, with wet washcloth.)

Did you know that the Bible is like a mirror? (Hold up Bible) When we read the Bible we can see what God wants our lives to look like. He gives us rules for how He wants us to live. Can any of you think of one of the rules God gives us in the Bible? (Children, obey your parents; You shall not lie; etc.) Our verse today asks the question, "How can a young man stay pure?" Or, "How can he clean up his life?" And the answer is given, "By reading [God's] Word and following its rules." Now think carefully a minute. Did the mirror wash my face off? No, I used a washcloth to do that. I could have said, I don't need to look in the mirror. Then I might never have known about all that jelly. Or, I could have looked in the mirror, seen the jelly, and decided not to do anything about what I saw. People sometimes treat their Bible-mirror that way, too. They decide they don't need to read the Bible, so they never learn about the wrong things in their lives. Other people do read the Bible sometimes, but they don't do anything about what they read. I guess they think that what the Bible says wasn't meant for them. But there are some people who do look into God's Word, and they see in that mirror the sin in their lives, and with God's help, they do something about it. Which kind of person are you?

Related Bible Story:

Daniel 1 (tell the story in your own words). Point to emphasize: It was because Daniel and his friends had been taught God's Word that they knew what food God wanted them to eat. God used them in a very special way because they tried to follow His teachings.

Activity: Draw self-portraits.

Materials:

As many mirrors as possible, ideally, one per child; one large piece newsprint per child; crayons.

Procedure:

Have the children take a good look at themselves in the mirror, then draw what they see. They can keep using the mirror as they draw. Note: Encourage children to use the mirrors by asking questions such as, "Are your ears higher or lower than your nose?", and so on.

3

A Measure (Two Lessons)

Suggested Song:

"Holy Bible, Book Divine"

Bible Verse:

"When they measure themselves by one another, and compare themselves with one another, they are without understanding" II Cor. 10:12b, RSV.

Object Lesson #1

Objects:

Strip of paper, 30″ long; specially prepared tape measure. (To do this, you will need to purchase two identical tape measures. From one tape measure, cut out a section from 29″ to 32½″. With tape, attach this section on top of the other tape measure between 25″ and 28½″. The tape measure should then read: 24″, 29″, 30″, 31″, 32″, 29″....

Did you ever hear anyone say, "But, Mom, everyone else gets to do it," or, "Mom, why can't I go? Marcie's going," or, "Why do I have to, *nobody* else does?" Does anyone you know ever talk that way? Do *you* ever talk that way? Do you know what people who say things like that are doing? They are using their own, or someone else's, idea of what is right as a measuring stick.

Let's try something with this tape measure. Joe, I'd like you to measure this strip of paper. Susan, please hold one end of the strip of paper together with the end of the tape measure which begins with one inch, two inches, three inches. That's right. Joe, you say the paper is thirty inches long? Thank you. Now, Susan, please carefully measure three inches from your end of the paper, and tear it off. Joe has found that the strip of paper was thirty inches long, and Susan has just torn three inches from the strip. Frank, how long will the strip of paper be now? You think it will be twenty-seven inches? Why don't you come and help me measure it? (Teacher holds end of paper strip together with the one inch, two inch, three inch end of the tape measure; Frank measures strip and finds it to be thirty-one inches long!) Thirty-one inches long! That's very strange, indeed. Thank you, Joe, Susan, and Frank. You may sit down now. I have to tell you something about this tape measure. I fixed it myself so the measurement would come out the way I planned it to.

There was once a little girl who took a small strip of paper (you can use the three-inch strip of paper which was torn off, and do this while you are talking), and she wrote 1, 2, 3, 4, 5, 6, 7, 8, 9, 10, 11, 12 on it. Then she measured herself with it. She ran excitedly to her mother, calling, "Mommy, Mommy! I'm taller than Goliath!" By *her* ruler, her measuring stick, she was more than nine feet tall, taller than Goliath. But do you think her measure was something to be trusted? No! Do you think the measuring tape I fixed up should be trusted?

God's Word, the Bible (hold up Bible), is a measure, too, and because it is *God's* word, we can trust what it says. Our verse in II Corinthians says that when people measure themselves by what other people around them are doing, instead of by God's measure, they are not wise. The Bible gives us God's plan for how we should live.

(For this object lesson, I am indebted to my father, Rev. Philip Foxwell.)

Object Lesson #2

Objects:

Four or five containers of contrasting sizes, all labeled "one cup"; several packages unsweetened Kool-Aid; water; sugar; spoons for stirring;

large pitchers or other containers for mixing; Kool-Aid recipe printed on blackboard or large piece of paper (copy from package); paper cups.

How would you like to make some Kool-Aid today? I think we have all the things we need, here—Kool-Aid mix, sugar, water, pitchers. (Divide children into groups of about four; be sure you have enough containers marked "one cup" to use one with each group. Have at least three groups.) I don't think it matters which measuring cup we use. They're all marked "one cup," after all. (Have groups of children make Kool-Aid, using recipe, and the various measuring containers. Let them taste the assorted Kool-Aids and make observations.) How did the Kool-Aid your group made taste, Sandra? Was it sour? You didn't get very much Kool-Aid, either, did you? What about your table, Stefanie? It tasted like sugar water? Peter, how was the Kool-Aid at your table? Pretty good? I'm glad somebody ended up with good Kool-Aid! Let's all have some of the Kool-Aid Peter's table made.

Do you think it's important to use the right measure? Yes, it certainly is. We had all kinds of trouble when we tried to make Kool-Aid with just any measure! The people who made the recipe for Kool-Aid intended for us to use a certain size measuring cup.

The Bible is the measure God intended for us to use (hold up Bible). But instead, a lot of people try to use their own ideas, or what somebody else does, as a measure. Did you ever hear someone say, "But, Mom, *nobody* else has to," or, "Mom, everybody in my class is going"? Do *you* ever talk that way? Our verse in II Corinthians says that when people measure themselves by what other people around them are doing, instead of with God's measure, they are not wise. God gave us the Bible to use as our measuring cup. When we try to use something else as our measure, our lives end up like sour, or watery, or oversweet Kool-Aid.

Related Bible Story:

Luke 12:15–21. The rich man was well provided for by his own standards—he had built large barns and filled them with food. He had many possessions. But he did not realize that in God's eyes this was not enough. By God's measuring stick he fell short, because he had not accepted God's provision for his eternal life.

Activity: Make a measuring stick.

Materials:

Rulers; pencils; crayons; strips of light cardboard or tagboard 6″ long
and about 2″ wide (one per child); (For younger children, have the strips
already marked off in inches—older children may do this themselves,
and may mark half inches in as well, if desired.)

Procedure:

Have children mark their "measures" into inches, using rulers. Have
them write, "God's Word is my measure," and color as desired.

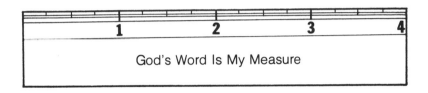

4

A Message

Suggested Songs:

"Holy Bible, Book Divine"; "Jesus Loves Even Me"

Bible Verse:

"I am come that they might have life" John 10:10b, KJV.

Objects:

Letters, addressed to each child. Preferably these should be mailed early in the week to the child's home, but be sure to have extras in case of visitors. If you don't mail the letters, have them ready to pass out as the children arrive. The letter should read:

> *Dear Sarah,*
> *I am glad you have been coming to our children's church. When you arrive on Sunday, look in the cabinet where the art supplies are kept [or some such suitable place]. There will be a little package for you, marked with your name. I am looking forward to seeing you on Sunday.*
>
> *Sincerely,*
> *Mrs. Loeks*

Wrap up a treat for each child. (I suggest the small, individual packages of raisins.) Print the child's name on the package. Be sure to have extras you can quickly fix up for visitors.

How many of you received a message in a letter this past week (or, as you came in the door this morning)? What did the message say? Who did what the message told you to do? What did you find? Peter, did you believe what the letter said? Why? (Because you knew and trusted the one who wrote it.)

The Bible is God's message to us. It tells us that God loves us, and it tells us about the gift of eternal life that Jesus came to bring us. We could decide that the letter isn't true, or isn't for us. Or, we can believe what it says, because we trust the one who sent the letter. That is a choice that you and I—everyone of us—have to make.

Related Bible Story:

Acts 8:26–39. Points to stress: The Ethiopian government official was reading from God's Word about how Jesus would have to suffer and die for our sin. God sent Philip to help explain what the Bible's message meant. The Ethiopian believed the message and became one of God's children.

Activity: Make a cross bookmark.

Materials:

Tagboard; paper punch; scissors; two yards yarn per child; tape; crayons.
Before the lesson the teacher should:
Cut out one cross per child from the tagboard. Use dimensions as shown in diagram. Using paper punch, punch holes around edges of cross, about ½" in from edge, and ½" apart. Tie end of yarn to cross at bottom corner. Wrap a piece of tape tightly around other end of yarn so it will go more easily through the holes.

Procedure:

Have each child print "God Loves You" on cross, then lace around the edges with the yarn. He may color it as he chooses. Each child may then choose someone to whom to give the bookmark.

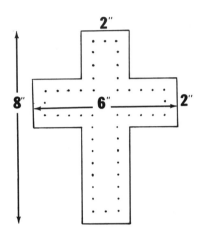

God Deals with Sin

5

Sometimes It Looks So Delicious!

Suggested Songs:

"What Can Wash Away My Sin?"; "Rolled Away"; "Gone, Gone, Gone, Gone, Yes, My Sins Are Gone."

Bible Verse:

"Satan himself masquerades as an angel of light" II Cor. 11:14b, NIV.

Object:

Mouse trap, set and baited with cheese. (Be sure bait is large enough that children can see it clearly and identify it.)

How many of you can think of some things that are dangerous? (Have children suggest objects.) Can any of you think of some things that are dangerous, but don't look that way at first? (Again have children make suggestions.) A lot of you have baby brothers or sisters. If a baby saw a shiny, sharp knife on the floor, he would think it was pretty, and fun to play with. He wouldn't know how dangerous its sharp edge really was.

Sin is a very dangerous thing to play around with, too. It is even more dangerous for you to play with sin than for a baby to play with a very sharp knife! Satan, who hates God, would like very much to have us play around with sin. The Bible says that sometimes Satan prowls around like a *roaring lion,* looking for someone to *devour!*

Sometimes, the sin that Satan would like us to play with also looks dangerous, just like a roaring lion. I don't think any of us would have trouble deciding if a lion who was roaring at us was dangerous, do you? But the Bible also says that sometimes Satan masquerades as, or pretends to be, an angel of light. An angel of light would seem to be a good thing, wouldn't it? And one of the tricks that Satan is best at, is convincing us to play with the sin that looks like a good thing at first.

This morning I brought a mousetrap with me. It's all set, and baited with the piece of cheese you see here. I brought this to show you because I think this trap is a lot like sin often is. Let's pretend this trap is all set in the corner of somebody's kitchen. At night, when it's dark and quiet, out comes Rodney the mouse. He smells the cheese, and he comes closer to the trap to check it out. He walks all around the trap. It smells so good! And it looks so good! Poor Rodney is terribly hungry. But Rodney knows that sometimes cheese like this can be very dangerous, if it has been put into a trap. Rodney has heard about traps from his aunts and uncles. So at first he is very cautious. Then, he takes just the teeniest of nibbles—and—nothing happens! And, oh, that cheese is so good! Rodney thinks to himself, "If I take this cheese back to my aunts and uncles and cousins, what a party we can have! What a celebration! And, parties are good things, aren't they? And sharing my cheese—isn't that a good thing, too?" Rodney begins to forget what his aunts and uncles have told him, and just as he is starting to take a big bite, SNAP! goes the trap! (Set off trap by poking with the eraser end of a pencil at the appropriate time.) And that is the end of poor Rodney.

Have you ever been like Rodney the mouse? I know I have been. I've let Satan trick me into thinking that some sin would be good for me, and good for other people. What can we do to keep us from being caught like Rodney? Do any of you have an idea? Yes, Joanne, studying the Bible is one of the best ways to learn which things are really good for us, and which things look good, but are really dangerous. Parents, teachers, and friends who love us and who love God can also help us to have a better idea of which things are truly good for us.

Related Bible Story:

Genesis 3. The serpent who tricked Eve was really a very beautiful animal. He convinced her that the fruit God had forbidden would really be a good thing for her.

Activity: Make a two-faced mask.

Materials:

8½ × 11 piece of construction paper per child; two 8″ pieces of string per child; scissors; miscellaneous scraps of construction paper; tape; glue.

Procedure:

Tell children they are to make a mask with a face on both sides. They may decorate the faces any way they please, but one side of the mask is to look as ugly as possible, and the other side as good and beautiful as possible. Tape the strings on either side of the mask to tie it on. Tell children that the two-faced mask is to remind them of Satan, who sometimes masquerades as an angel of light, and who tries to make a dangerous sin appear to be good and beautiful.

6

Forgiven Sin

Suggested Songs:

"Search Me, O God"; "What Can Wash Away My Sin?"; "Jesus Bids Us Shine"

Bible Verse:

"Blessed is he whose transgression is forgiven, whose sin is covered" Ps. 32:1, KJV.

Objects:

Flashlight, with miscellaneous items stuffed inside battery compartment of flashlight; working batteries (not in flashlight); red napkin or cloth of some kind.

(Flick the flashlight's on-off button a few times; shake it; tap it.) I have a flashlight here with me today, but I can't seem to make the light go on. It just doesn't seem to work properly. I can't figure out what's wrong. . . . I know! Maybe the batteries are worn out! I'll take a look and see. (Open flashlight battery compartment. Shake out the Cheerios, hair curler, tinker toy, kleenex, bottle cap, old sock, rusty nail—or whatever junk you have on hand.) My goodness! No wonder this flashlight wouldn't work.

This flashlight reminds me of some people I know. God wants us to be

His lights in this world. But we can't be a light that works if our lives are full of things that displease God—in other words, sins. Let's pretend this flashlight represents the life of a boy we'll call Jerry. (Pick up some of the items that were in the flashlight as you talk.) Jerry has a problem with a bad temper. And here are those little lies Jerry told so that no one would find out what a dumb thing he did last Tuesday. Then there was last Friday, when all the other kids on the block were buying popsicles, and he took some money out of his mother's wallet. That was stealing, wasn't it? And selfishness! Jerry wouldn't let his sister use his bike yesterday, even though he wasn't using it himself. Jerry always has a hard time sharing anything with someone else. Poor Jerry! What's he going to do about the sin in his life that keeps him from being the person God wants him to be? How are we going to get this flashlight working again?

The apostle John writes in his first letter, "If we confess our sins, He is faithful and just to forgive us our sins, and to cleanse us from all unrighteousness." And John says a few verses earlier in this same chapter, "The blood of Jesus Christ ... cleanseth us from all sin." Let's take this red napkin, and let it represent the blood of Jesus Christ who died on the cross for our sin. We'll cover up all these things that represent the sin in Jerry's life. (Wrap up, or cover all the items which were in the flashlight so that they cannot be seen). (Pick up the flashlight again, and flick on-off switch.) But this flashlight is empty, so it still doesn't work! It needs batteries, doesn't it? God doesn't leave our lives empty, either, boys and girls. He gives us Himself, His Holy Spirit to live within us, and be the power we need to let our light shine. (Put batteries in flashlight, and turn flashlight on.) Just as the flashlight needs the power of these batteries in order to give light, so Jerry and the rest of us need the power of the Holy Spirit in our lives to help us to be light for Him, and to be the kind of people God wants us to be.

Related Bible Story:

Luke 19:1–9. Zacchaeus confessed his sin to God and to those whom he had wronged. He did what he could to right the wrongs he had done. His sin was covered by what Jesus was going to do for Him on the cross. He was filled with the power of Jesus Christ, and could then be the light God wanted him to be.

Activity: Make a memory verse reminder.

Materials:

Crosses, cut from red construction paper, one per child (see dimensions on diagram); strips black construction paper, 8″ long by 2″ wide, one per child; pieces of white chalk; paste; tape; memory verse (Ps. 32:1) typed on strips of paper to paste on the cross, one per child.

Procedure:

Have children write "sin" on the black strip of paper with white chalk. Put the cross on top of the black strip of paper, and hinge together with a small piece of tape. Paste memory verse strip on cross. In this way, the cross "covers" the sin.

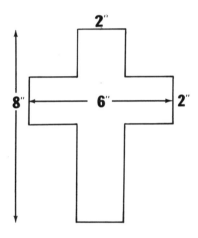

7

Sam's Heart House

Suggested Songs:

"Come Into My Heart, Lord Jesus"; "My Jesus, I Love Thee"

Bible Verse:

"Therefore, if anyone is in Christ, he is a new creation; the old has gone, the new has come!" II Cor. 5:17, NIV.

Object:

Poster with "Sam's Heart House" illustration (see directions on pp. 37-38).

I'd like to talk with you this morning about a boy named Sam, and the house he lived in. This is a picture of Sam's heart house. (Hold up poster).

Sam wasn't very happy about the way things were going at his heart house. He was having trouble taking care of it all by himself. One day, he heard a knock at the door. (Knock on a hard surface.) Sam called out, "Who's there?"

"Sam, this is Jesus," a voice said. "I know you've been having trouble with your heart house. I can help you, if you'll let me. Give me your house. Let me be completely in charge of it. Then I will be able to help you take care of the troubles you've been having."

Sam thought for a little bit. He really liked being in charge of his own house. He liked having his own name on the sign out in front. But he knew that he had been making a mess of things, so he decided to let Jesus take over.

He put a sign on the door that said, "Under New Management." Who knows what that means? Yes, it means that someone new is in charge. And even though it was hard for Sam to do, he changed the sign that said, "Sam's House" to read, "Jesus' House." (Attach new sign.) Jesus was now in charge of Sam's house. But Sam was like some people I know. Even though Jesus is supposed to be in charge of their lives, there are doors in their hearts they'd like to keep shut. But if Jesus is going to be in charge, He must be in charge of every room in the house.

Two of the rooms Sam opened up to Jesus right away were easy things for him to let Jesus be in charge of. (Open window covering penny; leave open.) He let Jesus be in charge of all his money. Now that would have been a much more difficult thing for Sam's dad to do, but Sam had very little money anyway, so it was quite easy for him to let Jesus be in charge.

And Sam opened this room up to Jesus right away. (Open window covering the desserts.) Sam didn't need to go on a diet, so he didn't have much problem letting Jesus be in charge of the food he ate. For Sam's mother, this would have been much more difficult.

The next room was Sam's "time room." Sam tried to discuss this with Jesus. He wanted to let Jesus be in charge of all of his time, *except* Saturday afternoons. On Saturday afternoon Sam wanted to be in charge of what he did with his time. Do you think this was all right with Jesus? Well, Jesus was very patient with Sam, just as He is with all His children. He never forces us to do things. But He kept reminding Sam of their agreement that He was to be in charge of the whole house, and finally, Sam opened that room to Jesus. (Open window covering clock.)

The next room was the room belonging to Sam's temper. Oh, could Sam get angry sometimes! "Jesus, you don't really want this room, do you? It's much better for me just to keep my bad temper locked up, don't you think?" But Jesus insisted that Sam open that door, too. (Open window covering lion roaring.)

The last two rooms were really hard ones for Sam to open up to Jesus. Jesus understood how hard this was for Sam, and He was very patient, but He didn't let Sam forget that He was to be in charge of all of the house. This room was the TV and book room. It represented the things

Sam put into his mind; the things he thought about. "I just can't give you this room, Jesus! It's just too hard for me. What if I give you all but this one closet?" But Jesus insisted on the closet, too, and finally Sam gave in, and opened that door to Jesus. (Open window covering TV and books.)

This last room had some of Sam's favorite things in it. Sam's new, ten-speed bicycle, his baseball glove, and his model airplane collection. He knew that if he gave up this room, Jesus would probably want him to share some of these prize possessions—and Sam didn't want to do that. Jesus didn't say much to Sam about opening the door—His being there, in charge of the other rooms of the house, was enough to remind Sam of what He had to do. So, finally, Sam opened that door too. (Open window covering bicycle, etc.)

Did you know that you have a "Heart House"? Perhaps some of the rooms in it are like rooms in Sam's House; probably you have some different rooms, too. Jesus wants very much to be completely in charge of your house, too. But He'll never break down the door, and push His way in. You have to be the one to open the door, and let Him be in charge.

Related Bible Story:

Acts 9:1-22. While focusing on the text, which deals with Paul's actual conversion experience, remind children of the kind of life Paul had led before (see Acts 7:58-60; those who were stoning Stephen put their outer garments at Saul's feet, thus indicating Saul's approval of Stephen's murder). Also, study Romans 5—7, where Paul relates something of the struggle he personally faces. Even Paul had to struggle to let Jesus really have control of every room of his "heart house." The solution for Paul, as it is for us, is in Jesus Christ, our Lord (see Rom. 7:24-25; 8:37-39).

Activity: Make a signpost.

Materials:

Two 12″ pipe cleaners per child; small lump of modeling clay per child; two 4″ by 1″ strips of cardboard per child, with II Corinthians 5:17 typed on one of the strips; tape; fine tip markers.

Procedure:

1) Have each child write "Jesus' House" on one cardboard strip, and "Joanne's House" (use own name) on the other strip. Have children hinge their two signs together with a strip of tape.

2) Double over one pipe cleaner and stick it into lump of clay to form signpost and base.

3) Twist one end of second pipe cleaner around signpost, and lay the hinged signs over this second pipe cleaner.

4) Fold the second pipe cleaner back over the signs, and twist the loose end around the signpost.

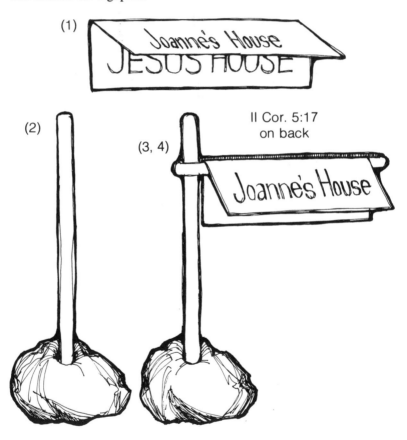

36

"Sam's Heart House" Poster:

Materials:

One standard size poster board; markers; scissors; tape; pictures from magazines; construction paper; penny or play money.

Procedure:

1) Locate and cut out pictures of the following in magazines: TV set and books; highly caloric food; roaring lion (or an angry person); clock; bicycle and other toys.
2) Cut out patterns for hearts by folding construction paper in half, and drawing one half of the heart, as shown. Cut on line.
3) Using markers, trace around heart patterns on the poster board background, making drawing similar to one on p. 38.
4) Cut out construction paper hearts to cover the "windows." Adjust the sizes of the heart-shapes to suit the size of the magazine pictures you have found.
5) Position the six pictures suggested above on the heart house, then tape or paste them in place on the poster. Cover the pictures with the heart-shaped window covers, and use tape as a hinge to hold the heart in place and to allow the window to be opened.
6) Cut out a heart from construction paper the same size as the one that says "Sam's House." On this heart, print "Jesus' House." Have tape ready to put this in place at the appropriate time.

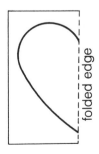

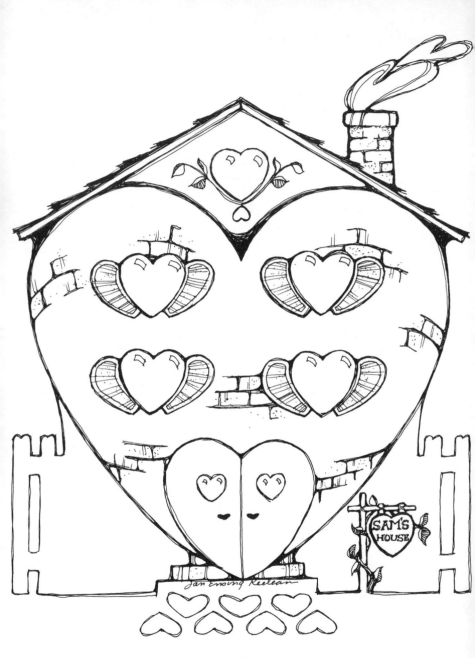

SAM'S HOUSE

Jesus, God's Son

8

The Most Important Christmas Gift

Suggested Songs:

"Thou Didst Leave Thy Throne"; other Christmas carols.

Bible Verse:

"The gift of God is eternal life in Christ Jesus our Lord" Rom. 6:23b, NIV.

Objects:

3 × 5 cards and pencils, one per child. Boxes, wrapped up as Christmas gifts, each containing a card with one of the following Scripture references:

John 14:16 (Comforter)	Matthew 11:29 (Yoke)
John 10:10 (Life)	Psalm 51:12 (Joy)
John 14:27 (Peace)	Isaiah 40:31 (Strength)
John 3:16 (Son)	John 14:2 (Place)
Isaiah 60:1a (Light)	Psalm 121:2 (Help)

Place boxes under a Christmas tree, if you have one.

A joyful Christmas to each one of you! Christmas is an exciting time of year. But sometimes, in all the excitement, we forget the most important gift ever given at Christmas. That gift is the gift God has given us. We have some gifts up here under the Christmas tree. Inside them are clues to what we receive by accepting the gift Jesus came to give us. I would like to have some of you come up now, and open these gifts, one at a time. They are gifts to each one of us, from Jesus. (Have two or three children at a time come up, select a gift, and open it. Have each child look up the Scripture reference in his or her Bible. Or, the text of the verses can be included on the Scripture reference card. Each child should read his verse and tell what the gift from God is. Repeat until all the gifts have been opened in this manner.)

The most important gift ever given to anyone is the gift of the Lord Jesus Christ: He gave Himself so that we could have eternal life. All of these other gifts that we have been discovering in the packages are part of this very wonderful gift of eternal life. Let's take time now, to thank God for His gifts to us. (Do so.)

I have one more package here. This box is empty. (Show children a gift-wrapped box with the lid and the bottom part of the box wrapped separately so box can be easily and quickly opened and closed.) I also brought with me some cards and some pencils. (Distribute these, one of each per child.) I'd like to invite you to think of something you can give to Jesus. It is His birthday, after all. As you think of what you can give, remember that Jesus said that doing something for someone in His family is like doing something for Him. When you've thought of what you can give, write it on the card, and come up and put it in the box. Remember, too, that the most important gift any of us can ever give Jesus is ourselves. He wants to be in charge of our whole lives. If any of you have never given that gift to Jesus, this would be a good time to do it. (Be sure teachers participate in this activity as well. Children will be much more likely to take it seriously.)

Related Bible Story:

Luke 2:1–20. Ask God to take this very familiar passage and make it real, first of all to you, so that you in turn can make it real to the children. This might be a good time to let the children act the story out.

Activity: A Birthday Party for Jesus.

Materials:

Cupcakes with candles for all the children.

Procedure:

Sing "Happy Birthday" to Jesus. Let children blow out candles. Have a party!

9

"It Is Finished"

Suggested Songs:

"My Jesus, I Love Thee"; "What Can Wash Away My Sin?"

Bible Verse:

"When he had received the drink, Jesus said, 'It is finished.' With that, he bowed his head and gave up his spirit" John 19:30, NIV.

Objects:

Two drawings; one complete, the other very obviously incomplete, but with the completed portion as much like the other as possible.

I have a picture I have been working on, and I wanted to bring it to show to you this morning. I'm interested in what you think of it. (Show half-completed drawing.) What do you think, Amy? (If it is obvious that the drawing is not finished, one of the children will probably make a comment to that effect.) Yes, Amy, you're right, this drawing isn't finished. I also brought another drawing to show you. This drawing is something like the first one, but this one is finished. What does it mean when a job you were supposed to do is finished? (Solicit answers.)
I brought these pictures to help remind us of something Jesus said. Perhaps it is the most important thing said in the entire Bible. Jesus had

come to earth to do a very important job. What was that job? Do you know, Wendy? Yes, the job was to die on the cross for our sins. And the most awful part of His dying on the cross was that He had to be separated from God the Father for a time. He cried out to God the Father, and God the Father didn't hear Him. Because Jesus allowed this to happen to Himself, we will never have to know what it means to be truly separated from God. If Jesus hadn't died for us, our sin would have kept us from ever being able to call on God's help. So this was the very important job that Jesus, the Son of God, came to do. It was a very terrible job, more terrible than any of us will ever fully be able to realize. But finally, Jesus knew that He had done what He had come to earth to do, and He was able to say, "It is finished."

Because Jesus finished the job, we know that God will hear us when we pray to Him. He will forgive us for our sin. He will help us with the hard things we have to face. And Jesus is preparing a special place in heaven where we can enjoy being with Him *forever*.

Related Bible Story:

The Crucifixion of Jesus. See particularly John 19:28–30, but study also John 19:16–27, Luke 23:26–49, Mark 15:21–41, Matthew 27:32–56. Jesus' death and separation from God was necessary to rebuild the bridge between ourselves and God that had been broken down by sin.

Activity:

Materials:

Crayons; glue; for each child, a sheet of paper on which has already been drawn a stick figure representing "me," and a symbol representing God (see illustration); for each child, a paper cross with the following verse typed on it: "The gift of God is eternal life through Christ Jesus our Lord" Romans 6:23.

Procedure:

Tell the children they need to "finish the picture" by drawing a bridge between "me" and God. The bridge should be labeled "Jesus." Have children paste the paper cross onto the picture. Have them label their drawing, "It is finished."

For this object lesson idea, I am indebted to Rev. Allan Baldwin, who used it with the children of Christ Church.

10

He Is Risen!

Suggested Songs:

"Christ the Lord Is Risen Today"; "Low in the Grave He Lay"; other Easter hymns.

Bible Verse:

"He is not here; he has risen, just as he said. Come and see the place where he lay" Matt. 28:6, NIV.

Objects:

A pot of blooming crocuses (or other flowers) and some crocus bulbs— if possible, enough for each child to take one home.

Who can tell me what these are? (Show children the crocus bulbs.) That's right, Kent, these are bulbs. They don't look very beautiful, do they? And they're pretty dead looking, too, aren't they? I brought these bulbs to show you today because they are the beginning part of a miracle. You usually put bulbs like this into the ground in the autumn. Then the ground freezes, and the snow falls and covers everything. Perhaps you even forget just where you planted the crocus bulbs. But in the spring, the miracle happens! Just as soon as the ground begins to warm up, up come some tiny green shoots. And soon the purple crocuses begin to bloom; just like the ones you see here in this pot. (Show pot of blooming crocuses.) God has done a miracle—something only He can do! He has turned dead-looking bulbs like these into beautiful crocuses.

The crocus miracle helps remind me of the most important miracle God ever did. Who can tell me what that was? Yes, Susan, when God made Jesus to be alive again, after He had died. That was His most important miracle. Because Jesus died and rose again we can be God's children now and forever. After we die, we will rise again and live forever with God in the place Jesus has prepared for us. That's why Jesus' resurrection is so important.

Today, Easter, is the day we have set aside to remember Jesus' resurrection. I'd like to give each one of you a crocus bulb to plant in a pot when you get home, so that the miracle of the crocus can help remind you, too, of God's most important miracle.

Related Bible Story:

Matthew 28:1–10. Perhaps if the children act this out it will help them recapture the drama and significance of the resurrection story. Help them to see the relevance of this event for their lives.

Activity: Plant a crocus bulb.

Materials:

Per child—styrofoam cup; crocus bulb; potting soil; typewritten strip of paper with Matthew 28:6 on it; some spoons and glue that children can share.

Procedure:

Using large spoons, put soil in the cup, put in the bulb, and cover with more soil. Glue Bible verse to outside of cup.

11

The Lord's Supper

Suggested Songs:

"My Jesus, I Love Thee"; "Sons of God"; "Christ the Lord Is Risen Today"

Bible Verse:

"This is my body, which is for you; do this in remembrance of me" I Cor. 11:24b, NIV)

Objects:

Glass of grape juice or wine; loaf of bread; American flag; picture of George Washington; birthday candles; Mothers' Day card; large calendar with special holidays indicated.

Why do we have holidays like the Fourth of July, or Mothers' Day, or George Washington's Birthday?* Do any of you have an idea? These special days have been set aside to help us remember someone special, or something very important that has happened. On George Washington's Birthday, we remember our country's first president. On Mothers' Day, we try to do special things for our mothers, don't we?

---

*Substitute suitable holidays and objects if lesson is used with children of another nationality.

49

We put birthday candles like these on a cake to celebrate the day that someone who is special to us was born.

There is a very special celebration that our church has on the first Sunday of every month [or whatever your church's custom is]. It is a celebration that Jesus asked us to have in order to help us remember Him, and what He did for us. Who can tell me what it was that Jesus did for us? That's right, Steve, Jesus died on the cross for our sins, didn't He? So when we celebrate the Lord's Supper, or Communion, as it is sometimes called, it is a very solemn and serious thing. We are reminding ourselves that Jesus was punished, and hurt far more than we will ever realize, so that we wouldn't have to be punished for our sin and for the wrong things we have done. We are responsible for Jesus' death.

Jesus asked that we use the juice of the grape, like you see here, to remind us of His blood. And He asked us to break bread, like this, to remind us of the way His body was given for us. The apostle Paul gave preachers a solemn warning to be sure that as people are invited to take part in the Lord's Supper, they truly understand what it means to be responsible for Jesus' death. So at our church, we think it is very important for children—and adults too—to have this kind of understanding before they show their love for Jesus by eating the bread, and drinking the juice.

But what can *everybody* who loves Jesus, even little people, do during the celebration of the Lord's Supper? It's a good time to tell Jesus that you love Him! It's a good time to tell Him a great big thank you! It's a good time to think of something you could do this week, to show Jesus that you love Him. And it's a good time to help the adults, and everybody, to remember that there's a joyful part to the Lord's Supper celebration, too. Sometimes I think some adults forget that part. While we are reminding ourselves that we are responsible for Jesus' death, we should also remind ourselves that Jesus didn't stay dead. He rose from the grave, and He's alive today. That is the joyous part of the Lord's Supper celebration! I think it would be good if we ended every celebration of the Lord's Supper by singing "Christ the Lord Is Risen Today: Alleluia!" Let's sing that together, now.

Related Bible Story:

Luke 22:1–20. We pattern our celebration of the Lord's Supper after this last supper that Jesus ate with His disciples before His death.

Activity:

Help the adults remember the joyful part of the Lord's Supper celebration. Practice singing "Christ the Lord Is Risen Today" (or some such hymn) in preparation for doing so during the next worship service when the Lord's Supper is celebrated.

God and His People

12

Safe Under His Wings

Suggested Songs:

"Safe Am I"; "O God, Our Help in Ages Past"; "Under His Wings"; "Jesus Keeps Me" (substitute "keeps" for "loves" in "Jesus Loves Me")

Bible Verse:

"He shall cover thee with his feathers, and under his wings shalt thou trust" Ps. 91:4a, KJV.

Object:

Picture of a mother hen and her chicks.

This morning I would like to tell you a story about a mother hen and her chicks. They probably looked quite a bit like the hen and chickens you see in the picture here. This chicken family lived quite happily in the henhouse that was part of a large farm. During the day, they would go out into the yard, and the mother hen would look for bits and pieces of things to eat, and to feed to her chicks. At night the hen family usually stayed in the henhouse. But one night, something very terrible happened. A fire started in the henhouse! Fire engines rushed screaming up to the farmhouse, and the fire was put out as quickly as possible. When the firemen went inside what was left of the henhouse, they discovered that the mother hen had died in the fire. But when the fire started, she had gathered her chicks tightly under her wings. All of the baby chickens were alive and well, because they had been kept safely under the mother hen's wings!

I'm not sure if this story ever really happened, but it is true that mother hens do a good job of taking care of, and protecting, their chicks. I told you the story because God is something like that mother hen! Of course, God is so big, and so great, it will take all of eternity before we know completely what He is like. But the Bible has given us some little pictures, to give us a hint of what God is like. One of the little pictures comes to us from King David. In one of his psalms, David said about God, "He shall cover thee with his feathers, and under his wings shalt thou trust." Jesus said about the Jewish people, "How often I have longed to gather your children together, as a hen gathers her chicks under her wings . . ." Matt. 23:37.

Mother hens do a good job of protecting their chicks. But God loves *us*—very, very much. That's something even a very good mother hen can't do! And because God loves us, He wants to take care of us and protect us. He wants His children to feel as safe with Him as baby chicks feel when they are under their mother's wings.

Related Bible Story:

Exodus 2:1-10. Even though the wicked pharaoh had cruelly ordered the death of all Israelite baby boys, God protected Moses and kept him safe, right under the pharaoh's nose!

Activity:

Materials:

Crayons; one sheet paper per child.

Procedure:

Have children talk about times when they are afraid—during a thunderstorm, when lost, alone on a dark night, and so on. Invite them to draw a picture of one of those times. Label the picture, "Jesus Keeps Me."

13

Hard Times

Suggested Song:

"Jesus Loves Even Me"; "For God So Loved the World"; "Jesus Loves Me."

Bible Verse:

"And we know that all things work together for good to them that love God, to them who are the called according to His purpose" Rom. 8:28, KJV.

Objects:

Container of flour; can of baking powder; can of shortening; cookies—one per child—wrapped in individual plastic bags and tied if they are not to be eaten right away.

Sometimes very hard things happen to us. People we love may get very sick. They may even die. Sometimes a mother and a daddy decide not to live together any more. Or perhaps we want something very badly, but we can't have it. Does God love us when these hard times come? Yes, He surely does, doesn't He, Sandy? But it's hard for us to remember that sometimes.

If I asked you what your favorite things to eat were, how many of you would choose baking powder? Have any of you ever tasted baking powder? Would you like to? How does it taste, Emily? By itself it doesn't taste very good, does it? (As time and interest permit, let the children taste the shortening and the flour as well). But you know, we couldn't have cookies like these you see here if it weren't for the baking powder, the flour, and the shortening.

These cookies have helped me understand a Bible verse I've always found difficult. Romans 8:28 says, "And we know that all things work together for good to them that love God, to them who are the called according to His purpose." The flour, the baking powder, and the shortening which don't taste very good by themselves all work together with the other ingredients to make a very good tasting cookie. (Distribute cookies to children at this point, or wait till later, as seems appropriate.)

We may not understand until we get to heaven why God lets certain hard things happen to us. But we know for sure that God loves us, and that He knows what He is doing. He won't put too much "baking powder" into our lives! If we love God, if we are His children, He will work together all the things that are part of our lives so that the end result will be a good one.

Related Bible Story:

Genesis 37, 45. When Joseph's brothers took his coat, and sold him as a slave, he may have had a hard time reminding himself that God loved him. He probably didn't see, then, how God could possibly work everything out for good. But God loved Joseph, and He knew what He was doing! He allowed Joseph to be taken to Egypt so that many people's lives could be saved, including the lives of Joseph's own family.

Activity: Make a puzzle.

Materials:

One piece of tagboard per child; one envelope per child (to put puzzle pieces in); crayons; scissors.

Procedure:

Print (or let the child print) today's verse on the tagboard. Have children draw a picture on the tagboard. Cut, or let them cut, the tagboard into ten to twelve pieces.

14

Giving Thanks

Suggested Songs:

"Thank You, Lord"; other songs expressing thanks to God.

Bible Verse:

"Give thanks in all circumstances, for this is God's will for you in Christ Jesus" I Thess. 5:18, NIV.

Object:

Dish of gumdrops, or other small candies.

(As children enter, greet them, and show them the dish of gumdrops, or other small candies. Invite each child to take a piece. The times that I know of that this has been tried, no one has said thank you! You will have to adapt your comments to the way your group of children responds.)

As you came in this morning, you (or some of you) reminded me of a group of lepers! Do you know why? (Allow children to guess.) I gave something to each one of you, and you (or some of you) forgot to say thank you! There were ten lepers in the Bible for whom Jesus did something very wonderful, and nine of those lepers were just as forgetful as some of you. (Go directly into the Bible story in Luke 17 at this point.)

* * *

The lepers certainly had something to thank God for. Can each one of you think of something that you can thank God for? (If possible, take the time to have each child share something for which he thanks God.) We've all mentioned things for which we can thank God. And we've all mentioned things that look to us to be good. But take a look at our Bible verse. It says, "Give thanks in all circumstances." What do you think "in all circumstances" means? What about the day your family had planned to go to the beach for a picnic, and it poured rain? Is that a circumstance in which we should be giving thanks? What about the time you were supposed to go to your best friend's birthday party, and you came down with the measles the day before? Is that a circumstance in which we should be giving thanks? I have to admit, I have an awfully hard time giving thanks when it looks to me like things are going wrong. But that's what the apostle Paul says we should be doing! Can any of you think of a really hard thing that you have to face, that we could give thanks about today? (If possible, share something from your own life.) Let's be like the one leper who remembered to say thank you, and let's give thanks to God, both for the things that look good to us, and for the hard things He's put into our lives. (Do so.)

Related Bible Story:

Luke 17:11–19. Jesus gave the lepers the gift of restored health—He took away their leprosy. But nine of the ten lepers went their way without even thanking Him.

Activity: Make a "thank-you" card.

Materials:

Construction paper; crayons; pencils (or felt-tipped pens); scraps of paper or cloth; glue.

61

Procedure:

Ask children to think of someone for whom they could make a "thank you" card. Let them design and put together their own cards with the materials you have supplied.

15

Trust

Suggested Song:

"Trust and Obey"

Bible Verses:

"Trust in him at all times" Ps. 62:8a, KJV. "Put all your trust in the Lord and do not rely on your own understanding" Prov. 3:5, NEB.

Objects:

Blindfold; chair; a small piece of candy.

This morning I need a volunteer. It must be someone who *really* trusts me. I am going to put a blindfold on him, and do some things with him, and ask him to do other things, and he must believe that I would not let anything harmful happen to him. Aaron, do you think you can trust me? Good. (Put blindfold on volunteer. Turn him completely around several times.) Aaron, please take ten steps in the direction you are now facing. (Be sure he can do so without bumping into anything.) Thank you. Now, would you please open your mouth? I have something small and hard I would like to put inside. (Put candy in child's mouth.) That's good. Now, I have put a chair just behind you. Please sit down in it. Thank you, Aaron. I appreciate your trust in me. Let's take that blindfold off. You may go back to your seat.

What does it mean to *trust* someone? Think about that question as you listen to the story I'm about to tell you. Have any of you ever seen a person walk on a tightrope? One time, a man stretched a tightrope across Niagara Falls. A large crowd gathered, and the man walked across the rope which was stretched over the falls. Then he took a bicycle, and rode the bicycle on the tightrope over the falls! When he got to the other side, the man asked the crowd a question. ''How many of you think I could carry another person across with me?'' he called out. A number of people in the crowd called back, ''Sure, try it. You can do it!'' The tightrope walker then asked, ''All right, which one of you wants to be carried first?'' Not a person answered! The people who said they believed he could carry someone didn't believe the tightrope walker enough to trust him with their own lives.

What do some of you think it means to trust someone? (Encourage children to share their thoughts.) I think that if you really trust someone, you are willing to go out on a tightrope with him. It means being willing to take a risk. Aaron trusted me this morning; he took a risk and believed that I wouldn't let anything hurt him, even though he couldn't see where he was going, or what I was doing.

Do you think we ought to trust everybody? Perhaps the people watching the tightrope walker were smart. It is foolish to put trust in something or someone who isn't *trustworthy*. The people and things we trust do sometimes disappoint us. But God will *never* disappoint us. God is completely worthy of our trust. We can trust him at all times, as our verse says. We can go out on the tightrope with Him, any time.

Related Bible Story:

Matthew 14:22-33. When Peter demonstrated his trust in Christ by keeping his eyes only on Christ, he was able to do what would otherwise be impossible. Peter walked on top of water in response to Jesus' invitation that he do so. Peter's trust faltered, however, as he looked around at the storm, and it was then that he began to sink.

Activity: Make a clock that tells what time God is trustworthy.

Materials:

Paper plate (for younger children, place dots where numbers on the clock face should go), one per child; brass paper fastener, one per child;

two clock hands cut from construction paper to fit size of plate; verse typed on piece of colored construction paper (Ps. 62:8a); glue; crayons; paper punch.

Procedure:

Use crayons to put numbers on paper plate to form clock face. Put brass fasteners through clock hands, and then through center of plate. Paste verse on center of clock face.

16

Why God Wants Us to Obey

Suggested Song:

"Trust and Obey"

Bible Verse:

"All that the Lord hath said will we do, and be obedient" Exod. 24:7b, KJV.

Object Lesson and Activity:

Try playing a game without obeying its rules. Use either "Mother, May I?," or "tic-tac-toe," if space and circumstances don't permit a more active game. To play "Mother, May I?" *with* rules, one person is the leader, or "Mother," and stands a certain distance away from the starting line. The rest of the players begin by standing on the line. "Mother" gives each player, in turn, an instruction about what kind of, and how many steps he may take in her direction (for example, two hops, three skips, four baby steps, or one giant step.) After "Mother" tells player what kind and how many steps he may take, the player must ask, "Mother, may I?" before taking the steps. If he forgets to ask, he loses his turn, and "Mother" gives instructions to the next player. The first player to reach "Mother" wins, and becomes the new "Mother." For tic-tac-toe, divide the children into pairs, and supply them with pencils and paper.

With either game, make sure that the rules of the game are clearly understood, and have children play the game correctly for a few minutes, following the rules. *Then* tell them they don't have to obey the rules any more. A baby step can be taken any way they wish, for example. They don't have to take turns. They don't have to remember to say, "Mother, may I?" And, who says there can be only one mother? The children may need some encouragement at first, to totally abandon all rules, but once they do, be prepared for tempers to flare, and for some children to become upset. At this point, call the children back to order. (A whistle is a good idea!) Have them be seated in a circle on the floor or ground. Give them time to sit down, and become quiet.

* * *

Do any of you have an idea why God asks us to obey His rules? (The children should have plenty of ideas by this time. Let them share them. It will help them to vent some of the hostility they may still be feeling!) Do you think God gave us rules just to be mean, and to show us how powerful He is? No, God gave us rules because He knew that by obeying them things would work out best for us. A game isn't any fun if we forget all about the rules, is it? God knew that if we did things in a certain way, and lived our lives in a certain way, we would be much happier. Because God loves us so very much, He gave us some instructions about how to live our lives. Who can tell me where a lot of God's instructions are written down? That's right, in the Bible. And God wants us to obey Him. The song we sang this morning says, "There's no other way to be happy in Jesus, but to trust and obey." Do you know that people who don't obey God are often very miserable? They are even more unhappy than some of you were when we tried to play "Mother, May I?" without obeying the rules of the game!
Let's try to play "Mother, May I?" again, only this time, let's obey the rules!

Related Bible Story:

Exodus 23:30–33; Joshua 9. God told the Israelites exactly what land they were to have. All the inhabitants were to be driven out, and they were to make no covenants with them. God warned that if these heathen people remained in the land, they would tempt the Israelites to sin. In

67

chapter 24 of Exodus we read that the Israelites assured Moses, "All that the Lord has said will we do, and be obedient." But Joshua 9 tells that the leaders of Israel, because they did not look to God for counsel, were tricked by the representatives of Gibeon into disobeying the Lord's command. This resulted in exactly the kind of problems God had warned them of in Exodus. This would be a good story for the children to act out if you have remaining time. Make this lesson relevant to the children by having them think of instructions God has given *them* to obey.

17

The Tongue

Suggested Songs:

"O For a Thousand Tongues to Sing"; other songs of praise to God

Bible Verse:

"The tongue also is a fire" James 3:6a, NIV.

Object:

A lit candle, or hurricane lamp with flame clearly showing, or, ideally, a fireplace with a fire lit in it, if this is possible. Optional: a recent news article, telling about a fire in your area.

In front of us this morning we have some fire. Who can think of some of the good things a fire can do? Yes, there's nothing like a fire on a cold winter night to keep us warm. A fire also gives us light, and it cooks our food. When a fire is under control, as it is in a fireplace, it is a beautiful thing to watch. But when a fire gets out of control, it is a most terrifying sight. Do any of you know someone whose house caught fire? I saw this article in the newspaper this last week. It's about a fire that destroyed a large part of a lumber yard [use facts from local paper]. Fire does many good things for us, but it can also do terrible things.

Can any of you think of some other bad things a fire does? Yes, Eileen, forest fires destroy trees, don't they? If you get too close to a fire, it will burn you.

There's a part of our body that the Bible compares to a fire. Do any of you know what that part is? The apostle James writes in the third chapter, verse 6, of his book that the tongue is a fire. I wonder why he wrote that. Do any of you have an idea? Can you think of some good things a tongue can do? A tongue can make someone feel good, by saying something like, "Thanks for the delicious breakfast, Mom." Or it can encourage someone, "I think you can do it, if you try just one more time." A tongue can praise God, as we did in our singing time this morning. A tongue can pray to God, or it can tell someone else about Jesus.

But a tongue can also say some very evil, hurtful things. It can tell lies. It can take God's name in vain, or swear. A tongue can gossip. Gossiping is passing on information that can hurt other people. People usually gossip because they like the attention they get by passing on exciting or shocking news. Often their "news" turns out to be only partly true, or perhaps not true at all. I know of some times when gossip has caused every bit as much destruction and pain as the burn from a fire. I think that James gave us a good object lesson when he said that the tongue is a fire. Our tongues can do a great deal of good, if we let them. But they can also do a great deal of terrible damage, if we don't keep them under control.

Related Bible Story:

Acts 16:16–34. Paul and Silas used their tongues to sing praises to God, even while they were in jail. They also used their tongues to tell the jailor how he could become God's child.

Activity: Toast marshmallows.

Materials:

Marshmallows; skewers (make them from wire coat hangers if you don't have enough); fireplace, grill, or bonfire.

Procedure:

Allow fire in fireplace to die down to glowing embers, or take the children outside, where a bonfire or charcoal grill ready to toast marshmallows has been prepared.

As you toast and eat your marshmallows, remind children that toasting marshmallows is one of the good things that fire does. Encourage them to think of, and share, good ways in which they can use their tongues this week.

18

Good Medicine

Suggested Songs:

"I Have the Joy, Joy, Joy, Joy''; "Jesus Bids Us Shine"

Bible Verse:

"A cheerful heart does good like medicine" Prov. 17:22a, LB.

Objects:

Several medicine bottles; a large paper heart with the symbol for prescription (℞) and a happy face drawn on it.

How many of your parents let you get into the medicine cabinet whenever you want to, let you play with medicines, and let you give them to your friends whenever you wish? I doubt any of your parents would let you do that! But there is one kind of medicine talked about in the Book of Proverbs which I think anyone would be delighted for you to have, and to give large doses of to the people around you. Do any of you know what that is? (Show paper heart.) The medicine I'm talking about is a cheerful heart! Proverbs 17:22a, our verse for today, says, "A cheerful heart does good like medicine!" Do any of you know anyone who is sick today? Is there anything you can do to make that person happy? (Let children make suggestions.) What about when your mom or dad has had a hard day? What do you think would happen, if, when you were asked to clear the table, or help wipe the dishes, instead of whining, "Aw, Mom, do I have to?", you said with a big smile, "Sure, Mom!"? Yes, Robert, I think you're right, some of your mothers would be a bit surprised—but it would be a pleasant surprise for them! There's a special thing about "cheerful heart medicine"—it's contagious. Do any of you know what that word means? It means that other people can easily catch it. If you start out with a cheerful heart, other people are likely to catch it from you!

Let's all give out big doses of "cheerful heart medicine" this week!

Suggested Bible Story:

Acts 9:36–43. While Scripture doesn't specifically state that Dorcas had "a cheerful heart," her activities are a demonstration of this. God honored this faithful woman, and empowered Peter to do a miracle, and raise her from the dead.

Activity: Make a "cheerful heart" reminder.

Materials:

Construction paper heart with a hole punched in the top, one per child; piece of yarn 8″ long, one per child; strip of paper with Proverbs 17:22a typed on it, one per child; crayons; glue.

Procedure:

Have children draw a happy face on the heart. Put yarn through hole and tie it (to hang picture with). Paste verse on heart.

19

God Uses Little Gifts
from Little People

Suggested Songs:

"Take My Life, and Let It Be''; "What Can I Give Jesus?''

Bible Verse:

"So whether you eat or drink or whatever you do, do it all for the glory of God" I Cor. 10:31, NIV.

Objects:

Brown paper lunch sack containing a tuna fish sandwich; stack of books whose total number of pages come to about five thousand.

Julie, what do you think is in this bag? Why don't you take a look, and show us all what's inside? A tuna fish sandwich! Robert, how many people do you think could have lunch with what Julie found in this bag? I think you're right, probably just one person. The Bible tells us about a lunch almost like this one. In John, chapter 6, Jesus was teaching, and a huge crowd gathered. Because Jesus was famous for His teaching and doing miracles, the people had walked quite a distance from their homes. It got to be late in the day—time to eat—but nobody had brought any food along. That was particularly bad because in Jesus day there weren't any McDonalds or Burger Kings for the people to stop at. Nobody had brought any food, *except* for one young boy. He had brought five small loaves of barley bread and two little fish—just enough for one boy's lunch. But instead of going off behind a tree and eating it all by himself, he took that lunch and gave it to Jesus! It wasn't a very big gift, was it? But because it was a gift given to *Jesus,* Jesus did a miracle with it. He did something you or I could never do. Jesus took one little lunch—just about like this tuna sandwich—and with it He fed that whole crowd of people. Someone counted five thousand men there that day, and there were also many women and children. Do you know how many five thousand is? Look at this pile of books. All of these books, added together, have about five thousand pages in them. If we pretend that each page represents one man, that's how many men Jesus fed that day! And after all the people had had a good lunch, the disciples collected twelve big baskets of leftovers! Jesus took a little gift from a young boy, and did a wonderful miracle with it.

Related Bible Story:

II Kings 5:1–15. The Israelite maid was not very old, and not very important (her name is not even given in the Bible). But she had an important gift. Her gift was a message. She shared her faith in God and told of the prophet Elisha, who, with God's power, could heal Naaman of his leprosy.

Activity: Make a coat hanger mobile.

Materials:

One wire coat hanger per child; yarn strips per child—6 strips of 8″, 3 strips of 26″, 2 strips of 32″; for each child—12 basket shapes cut from brown construction paper, one "fed 5000" shape from bright orange or red paper, two fish cut from light green construction paper, five loaf shapes cut from light brown construction paper (these should be cut in advance, using patterns provided); crayons; rulers, or other measuring devices.

Procedure:

See accompanying diagram which shows how mobile should be assembled. Draw the diagram on a blackboard, or make a sample mobile. To

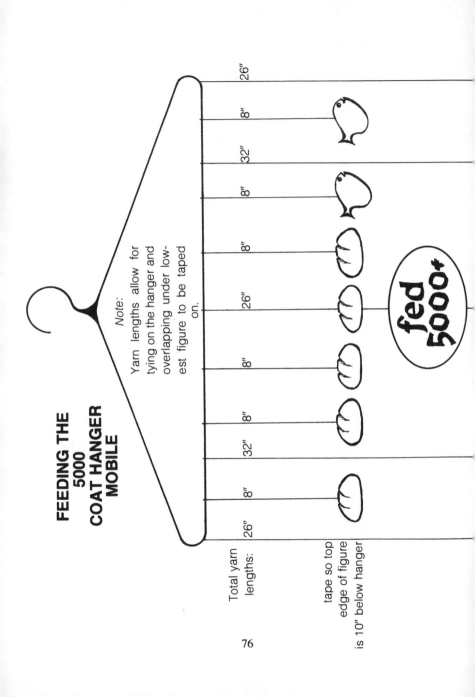

FEEDING THE
5000
COAT HANGER
MOBILE

Note:
Yarn lengths allow for tying on the hanger and overlapping under lowest figure to be taped on.

Total yarn lengths:

26"   8"   32"   8"   26"   8"   8"   26"   8"   32"   8"

tape so top edge of figure is 10" below hanger

fed 5000+

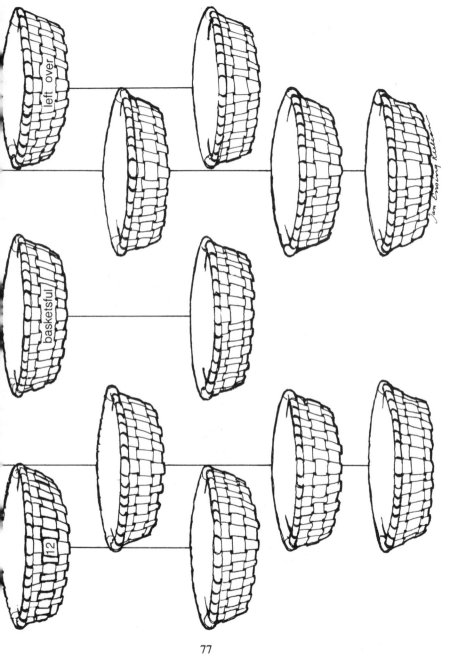

Patterns for Mobile Shapes (actual size)

need 2 per child

fed 5000+

need one per child

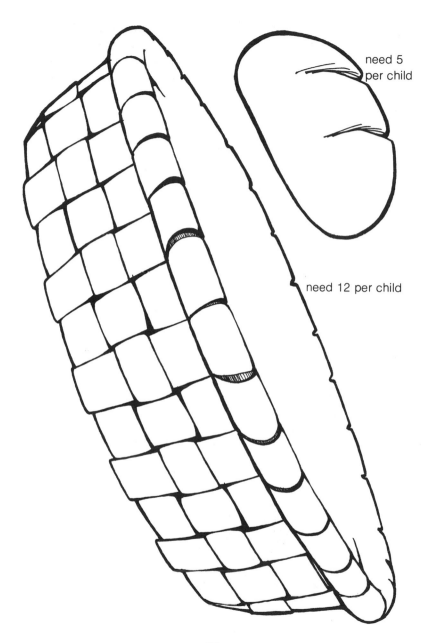

need 5 per child

need 12 per child

begin, have the children take their short (8″) pieces of yarn, and tape four of the loaves and the two fish to the very ends of the yarn pieces. The children can use their crayons to decorate these as well as the other shapes. Adult assistants can help the children assemble the remainder of the mobile.

Note: Ask additional adults to help, both in the preparation and the execution of this activity. This activity will take a little longer, so allow extra time, or else plan it for two class periods. We found that assembling these on the floor worked out well (there wasn't enough table space for all the children, once they began to assemble the mobiles.) Let each child have his own "piece of floor" to work on.

The Holy Spirit

20

The Fruit of the Spirit

Suggested Songs:

"Come, Thou Almighty King" (especially the third verse); "Come, Holy Spirit, Come." It is difficult to find songs on the Holy Spirit with words that can be understood by young children. There are several suitable songs in *The Children's Hymnbook* (Grand Rapids: National Union of Christian Schools and Eerdmans, 1962).

Come, Holy Spirit, Come

1 Come, Holy Spirit, come;
  Oh, hear my humble prayer!
  Stoop down and make my heart Thy home,
  And shed Thy blessing there.

2 Thy light, Thy love impart
  And let it ever be
  A holy, humble, happy heart,
  A dwelling place for Thee.

3 Let Thy rich grace increase,
  Through all my earthly days,
  The fruits of righteousness and peace,
  To Thine eternal praise.

Bible Verse:

"But the fruit of the Spirit is love, joy, peace, patience, kindness, goodness, faithfulness, gentleness and self-control" Gal. 5:22, 32a, RSV.

Objects:

Three clear glasses, preferably tall, narrow ones. One glass should be about half full of clear cooking oil, and should be labeled, "Holy Spirit." The second glass should be about half full of water, colored with blue or green food coloring, and the glass should be labeled, "Sin." The third glass should be left empty, and should be labeled "Gladys." You will also need something to stir with.

In the Old Testament times, oil was a symbol of the presence of the Holy Spirit. Kings, and others, had their heads anointed with oil as a symbol that the Holy Spirit was going to be with them in the job they had been given to do. I Samuel 16:13 is a good example of this: "Then Samuel took the horn of oil, and anointed [David] in the midst of his brethren: and the Spirit of the Lord came upon David from that day forward."

I have brought with me some clear oil in this glass that you see here, and we will let the oil represent the Holy Spirit, and the fruit of the Spirit. "Fruit of the Spirit" means what a person's life will be like when the Holy Spirit lives there. Paul describes this in Galatians 5:22–23: "the fruit of the Spirit is love, joy, peace, patience, kindness, goodness, faithfulness, gentleness and self-control." We'll let the colored water in this glass represent sin, and this empty glass we will pretend represents the life of a girl named Gladys. Gladys loves Jesus, and knows Him to be her Savior. She has the Holy Spirit living inside her. (Pour oil into empty glass). But Gladys wanted to watch a special program on TV.* Her mother told her that she could, if her homework was done. When it

*Use examples suited to the age level of the children you are speaking to. Specific examples of situations the children are likely to face are better than referring to general terms such as "dishonesty" or "jealousy."

was time for the program to start Gladys told her mother, "My homework is all done, Mom," even though she hadn't even started it! That was a lie, wasn't it? We'll put in some of this water, to represent Gladys's lie. (Pour some of colored water into 'Gladys' glass.) Gladys's neighbors down the street had a swimming pool, but Gladys's family didn't have one. Gladys was very jealous. (Add more colored water to 'Gladys.') Susan, the girl whose family had the swimming pool, invited other kids to go swimming, but she never invited Gladys. "If that's the way she's going to be, I don't care! I hate her, anyway!" Gladys stormed. (Pour remainder of colored water into Gladys's glass, and stir.) What happens when someone who has the Holy Spirit living inside her tries to mix sin with the fruit of the Holy Spirit? Let's watch and see! The clear oil of the Holy Spirit can't mix with the colored water, can it, no matter how we try to stir it! Sin in the life of a Christian doesn't mix well, either. But look! The oil, representing the Holy Spirit, always ends up on top, after it has separated itself from the water! When we ask for forgiveness, our sins are blotted out, and God sees the fruit of the Holy Spirit in our lives, not the sins.

Related Bible Story:

Acts 2. The Coming of the Holy Spirit. The Holy Spirit is God, and has always existed, just as God has. But Jesus promised, before He returned to Heaven, that He would send the Holy Spirit to be a Helper to Christians. The Bible story today tells about that special day (Pentecost) when the Holy Spirit came in a very special way to become part of the lives of those who were followers of Jesus. Ever since Pentecost, everyone who is God's true child has the Holy Spirit living within him, to be a Helper.

Activity: Make a memory verse reminder.

Materials:

Nine purple circles per child (cut them the size of a small juice glass); grape leaves cut from green construction paper, two per child; markers or crayons; glue.

Procedure:

Have the children write "love, joy, peace, patience, kindness, good-ness, faithfulness, gentleness, self control," one word in each purple circle. Then have them glue the circles together to form a cluster of grapes. Glue grape leaves on top. Write "The fruit of the Spirit" inside one leaf, and Gal. 5:22–23a inside the other.

21

A Seal

Suggested Songs:

"Come, Thou Almighty King"; "Come, Holy Spirit, Come"; (see note under last lesson)

Bible Verse:

"When you believed, you were marked with a seal, the promised Holy Spirit" Ephesians 1:13b, NIV.

Objects:

An Oriental painting or piece of art signed with two seals; a check made out to you; a "promissory note" for each child (see below); chocolate chip cookie (individually wrapped) for each child.

If you found a piece of paper on the floor in a large shopping mall that said, "I will give a free trip to Disney World and a week on the beach in Florida to whoever claims this paper," what would you think? Would you think anyone meant to keep that promise? Why not, Kristin? That's right, if there's no name, or signature, it's not likely that anyone intends to keep the promise. In many countries today, a signature lets us know who is responsible for what is on a piece of paper, and that he intends to do what he says he will do.

But in some countries today, such as Japan, people use a special seal, or stamp, in the same way that we would use our signatures. Every family has its own seal, and all important papers, as well as works of art, are signed with this seal.

I have brought with me a print by a Japanese artist. (Show it.) Can you see his seal, down here in the corner? But look carefully! How many seals do you see? Yes, there are two seals! It used to be the custom not only for the artist to "seal" his work, but also for the one who became the owner to put his seal on it as well. This second seal was as if to say, "I claim this piece of art. It belongs to me."

The apostle Paul says in Ephesians 1:13 that the Holy Spirit is *God's seal*. What do you suppose Paul meant when he wrote that? God has given us many promises in the Bible. He has also given us His seal, the Holy Spirit, to remind us who made the promises, and to let us know He intends to do what He has promised.

Remember that I told you that in Japan every family has its own seal. There is a very special sense in which the Holy Spirit is also the seal of those of us who are God's children, and members of God's family. It is the Holy Spirit who helps us to say, "I claim God's promises. They belong to me."

In the United States, owners don't sign their art, but we do something a little like that when we use checks. I have a check with me this morning that my brother has written and signed. He is asking his bank to pay me ten dollars. But before I can get that ten dollars, there is something I must do. Do any of you know what that is? Yes, Danny, I must put my signature on the back side of the check to say, "Yes, I claim this ten dollars." In the same way, if we want to receive God's very wonderful promises to us we must claim them, by the help of the Holy Spirit.

To help you remember how God's seal, and our seal, the Holy Spirit, helps us, I have something for you. [Distribute a "promissory note" to each child which reads: "I promise to give to the bearer one chocolate chip cookie following the morning worship service (or some other appropriate time) on ⎯⎯⎯⎯⎯⎯⎯⎯⎯⎯⎯⎯⎯⎯⎯⎯⎯

(date)

Signed: ⎯⎯⎯⎯⎯⎯⎯⎯ (your signature) ⎯⎯⎯⎯⎯⎯⎯⎯

Signature of bearer: ⎯⎯⎯⎯⎯⎯⎯⎯⎯⎯⎯⎯⎯⎯

(The bearer is the
one who claims this promise.)"]

You could do several things with this note. You could decide that I'm just kidding, that I don't really intend to do what I said I would, and you could throw this note away. Or, you could put the note in your wallet, and forget about it for a while. Or, you could sign the note with your signature, and come up later to claim the promise.

Related Bible Story:

Daniel 6. We can be pretty sure that King Darius signed the decree with his royal seal. The king's seal on the proclamation meant that he had to keep his promise, even though he feared that to do so would destroy his trusted subject, Daniel.

Activity: Make a seal.

Materials:

One 5-inch square of thick cardboard per child; one 5-inch square of newsprint per child; thick yarn (the kind sometimes used for gift wrapping); glue; crayons; tempera paint in foil pie pans; newsprint; scissors.

Procedure:

Children should use crayons to design seals for themselves on the 5-inch square of newsprint. They may use their initials, or make any kind of seal they please. Then they may draw their design on the cardboard, but *remind them that all letters must be done in reverse.* Check each child's cardboard to be sure this is done. Then allow children to glue the yarn over the lines they have crayoned. Let glue dry. Then children can use their "seals" to print with tempera paint on the newsprint. They should allow only the yarn to get into the paint.

The Church and Missions

22

You Are an Important Link

Suggested Songs:

"They'll Know We Are Christians by Our Love"; "What Can I Give Jesus?"

Bible Verse:

"But you are Christ's body and members with assigned parts" I Cor. 12:27, Berk.

Objects:

A wagon, a chain (preferably silver in color) with a middle link made of aluminum foil.

Missy, how would you like to hop in the wagon for a ride this morning? (Select a small child.) I am going to put this chain through the wagon handle. (Try not to let the aluminum foil link be too obvious.) Which of you thinks that he could pull the wagon with this chain? All right, Joe, come on up here, and take hold of these two ends of chain. Let's see if you can pull the wagon. (He attempts to pull, and the aluminum foil link breaks.) Missy, it looks like the chain is broken, I guess you won't get a ride, after all. What do you think happened, Joe? The chain *looked* like it was strong enough. (Point out the foil link, if the children haven't already noticed it.) One link of this chain was made of foil! Just one link, yet it kept the whole chain from doing its job.

Each one of us who is a child of God is like a link of a chain. If even *one* of us is not doing the job God has given us, or if we have sin in our lives we have not confessed to Him, we will keep the whole "chain" from doing its job. Every single link of the chain is very, very important.

Related Bible Story:

Joshua 7. Point to stress: Because one man, Achan, disobeyed God and kept some of the things God had told Israel to destroy, all the people suffered, and Israel was defeated at Ai.

Activity: Make a chain.

Materials:

Crayons; glue or tape; eleven strips of construction paper per child.

Procedure:

Have children print one word of the memory verse on each of the eleven strips. Link the strips in the correct sequence with tape or glue, forming a chain. (Younger children may need help to get links in correct sequence. They may also need help printing the words on the strips of paper.)

23

You Are Light

Suggested Songs:

"Jesus Bids Us Shine''; "This Little Light of Mine''

Bible Verse:

"You are the light of the world'' Matt. 5:14a, RSV.

Objects:

Candle; candle holder; matches; bowl or other non-inflammable object with which to cover lit candle.

How many of you ever use candles at your house? What is a candle supposed to do? Yes, a candle's job is to give light. (Light candle.) Sometimes, during a storm or power shortage, our houses are without electricity. When the sun goes down, and everything grows dark, what do we do? We light candles. We should all be very thankful for the light that the candles provide.

What would you think of a person who lit a candle, and then covered it with a bowl, like this? (Cover the lit candle.) You'd think he was a little bit silly, wouldn't you? Jesus said, "No one lights a lamp, and puts it in a place where it will be hidden, or under a bowl. Instead, he puts it on its stand, so that those who come in may see the light.'' (Place candle in candle holder) But, do you know, there are some people who are just that silly! Just before Jesus talked about how no one would hide a light after it was lit, he said, "You are the light of the world." Who was Jesus talking to? Everyone who is a child of God, who loves Jesus, is supposed to be the light of the world. But sometimes we're afraid of what other people might think of us. We're afraid they might not understand. We tell ourselves that somebody else could do a better job of being a light than we could. And we hide our light under a bowl! Jesus has asked us to let our lights shine, so that the people around us may see the good we do, and then they, too, will glorify our heavenly Father.

Related Bible Story:

Acts 10. God gave Peter a very unusual vision, to teach him that he was to be light to the Gentiles (non-Jewish people). He was not to hide his light under a bowl, but to share it with Cornelius and his family.

Activity: Make a candle holder.

Materials:

One glass bottle per child (coke, syrup, salad dressing, ketchup—anything with a neck into which a standard size candle will fit); small pieces of multicolored tissue paper. (If you have time, provide scissors and let the children cut their own); candle; glue; can of spray varnish; slip of paper with Matthew 5:14a typed on it, one per child.

Procedure:

Glue pieces of tissue paper so that the entire outside surface of the bottle is covered. The pieces of tissue paper should slightly overlap each other; this will allow the colors to blend. Smooth the tissue down to get rid of excess glue and air. Glue on the Bible verse strip. Allow to dry *thoroughly*. Spray with varnish. Stick candle in top of bottle.

24

You Are a Steward

Suggested Songs:

"The Wise May Bring Their Learning" (*The Children's Hymnbook,* p. 164); "Now I Belong to Jesus"; "What Can I Give Jesus?"

Bible Verse:

"You are not your own; you were bought at a price. Therefore honor God with your body" I Cor. 6:19b, 20, NIV.

Objects:

A clock; a large paper heart; a pair of cut-out paper feet; a pair of cut-out paper hands; an envelope containing an accumulated offering the children have given.

(Have several children, selected beforehand, come forward with the objects suggested above.) Good Morning, stewards! Thank you. Why do you suppose I called you "stewards"? How many of you know what a steward is? People who have traveled across the ocean on a big ship or ocean liner become acquainted with ship workers who are called *stewards*. The stewards make sure that everything on the ship is kept in good order. They serve meals in the dining room, and serve snacks in between meals. If anyone needs clean towels or sheets, all he has to do is ask the steward for them. The stewards supply ping-pong balls and paddles, or shuffleboard equipment for anyone who wants to play. Stewards bring out deck chairs for anyone wishing to sit out on the deck and watch the water. Now, I have a question for you. Do you think the stewards own the ship? No, the stewards do not own the ship, or any of the things on it. The owner of the ship puts the stewards in charge of taking care of all the things on the ship.

I called you "stewards" this morning because everybody who belongs to Jesus and who is one of God's children is a steward. All that we are, and all that we have, belongs to God. But God has given every one of us some things to be in charge of, for a while. We forget this, sometimes, and we say things like, "That's my boat, or my bike, or my money, or my time, or my body." But these are really things that we are stewards over. Just as the owners of the ship expect their stewards to use the things on the ship wisely, and take good care of them, so God expects us to take good care of, and use well, all that He has trusted us with.

Some of you brought up some things that remind you of what God has made you stewards of. David, you have brought a clock. God has made us stewards of our time. We are to use it wisely. Michael, you brought up the offering money we have been collecting this past summer to send to _____. God has made us stewards of our money. God has put us in charge of our hands and our feet, like those Emily and Rachel have brought. We can let our hands and our feet do those things which would please God, or we can let them do things which are not pleasing to Him. We are stewards of our hearts. We can choose to love God the most, or we can love some other person, or some other thing the most.

Let's not forget that we are God's stewards. As our verse says, we are not our own; we were bought with a price.

Related Bible Story:

Matthew 25:14–30. The owner entrusted his servants with some of his money while he went away. He expected the servants to use the money wisely, and make good investments for him. Two of the servants were "good stewards"; one was not. God wants us to use what He has entrusted us with for Him.

Activity: Make a stewardship reminder.

Materials:

One piece of white or light-colored construction paper per child; crayons.

Procedure:

Have each child write "Steward Aaron" (using his own name) at top of paper. Then have him draw a picture of something God has made him a steward over.

25

Sharing the Good News

Suggested Songs:

"Jesus Loves the Little Children"; "Jesus Loves You" (Substitute "you" for "me", and "the Bible tells *us* so"); "Go, Tell It on the Mountain"; "For God So Loved the World"

Bible Verse:

"For God so loved the world that he gave his one and only Son, that whoever believes in him shall not perish but have eternal life" John 3:16, NIV.

Objects:

Bright colored pennants, with "God Loves You" written in a different language on each one. If you can locate photographs of missionaries in whom your church is interested, place them on the pennant with the appropriate language.

What do you think a missionary's job is? Missionaries do lots of different things. Some are doctors and nurses, some translate the Bible into other languages, some teach, some preach, some help make radio and TV broadcasts, some take care of children in orphanages, and there are many, many, other things as well. But the main job of a missionary is telling other people, "God Loves You."

The writing that you see on these pennants is in different languages. Let me read some of them to you. (Do so.) But the message on each pennant is the same—"God loves you." That's a very important message. It is *the* most important message anyone will ever receive.

We usually think of missionaries as people who go to other countries to tell people that God loves them, but we can be missionaries, too. That's right, Bonnie, we can be missionaries right where we are by sharing with the people around us the good news that God loves them. We can tell them about the most important way in which God showed His love; by sending His Son, Jesus, to give His life for us.

Related Bible Story:

Acts 1:8, 10; Matthew 28:16–20. Sometimes, a great deal of significance is attached to a person's last words. Jesus' last words to His disciples before His ascension into Heaven were for them to tell others what they had seen and experienced of God's love for them.

Activity: Make a pennant prayer reminder.

Materials:

One per child—triangular-shaped pennant, cut from colored construction paper; missionary prayer-reminder card, with the missionary's photograph on it (these usually can be acquired from mission boards or agencies, or from the missionaries themselves); slip of paper with "God Loves You" typed in the language spoken in the country of the missionary on the child's prayer reminder card; a drinking straw; tape; glue; crayons.

Procedure:

Attach straw to construction paper pennant with scotch tape, to form a handle. Glue prayer reminder card and strip with "God Loves You" onto the pennant. Have children write (in English) "God loves you" on their pennant. The pennant is a reminder to pray for the missionary pictured, and to *be* a missionary, by telling others that "God loves you."